Make Music

A book of musical experiments for young people

Holmes McDougall Limited Edinburgh Glasgow London

Credits

Author: A Richard Addison, BA, MMus, LRAM.

School of Education, University of Newcastle-upon-Tyne

Art and design: Gillian Humphrys

Set in 10 point Univers with titling in Clarendon

Printed by Holmes McDougall Limited, Perth.

Published by Holmes McDougall Limited,

30 Royal Terrace, Edinburgh

ISBN 7157 0502-4

Contents

SX JERSE
BRAN

Household instruments

Here are some everyday things that you can use as musical instruments:

Bongo Drums from empty tins or an old kettle.

Shakers from plastic bottles with a little rice, sugar, lentils, or dried peas inside.

Bass Drum from a wooden vegetable tub or a large empty tin.

Cymbal from an old frying pan.

Bells from shelf brackets, or angle irons (ask Daddy), one of which is hung on a string.

Claves from two pieces of hard wood, of the same size.

Xylophone from different size flowerpots, hung upside down by a rope with a knot in the end.

Beaters for Bass Drum and Cymbal from a length of wood with cloth tied tightly round one end.

Keep a look out for other everyday things that would do for musical instruments.

If you collect some of these instruments at school, try to sort them into sets, each making a different *kind* of sound :–

There should be four sets :–

Those that *ring*

Those that *bang*

Those that *shake* or *rattle*

Those that *click*

Write four lists.

Home made instruments

Here are a few instruments you could very easily make.

Guiro: bamboo stick with little notches cut every half inch. Drag a large nail over the notches.

Hanging Xylophone: rather like a rope ladder. Use hard wood, and make each rung shorter than the one below it. Drag a piece of wood down it.

Clappers: a coconut cut in half and hollowed out. (Get your Dad to do the cutting for you.)

Glockenspiel: tumblers with different amounts of water in them.

Sandpaper Blocks: two blocks of wood covered with sandpaper.

Shaker: a piece of wood with 6 nails hammered half in, about 2 inches apart. Put milk bottle tops over the nails. To play, hold it with one hand and tap it with the other.

Can you put these instruments into the sets you made up with the household objects?

If you have triangles, tambourines, drums, cymbals, castanets or jingle bells in your school, which sets would you put them in?

Draw a picture of the sets, or arrange the instruments on a table, or write lists of the sets.

Body sounds

See how many different kinds of **clapping** sound you can make.

You should find at least four.

How many different sounds can you make with your **mouth**?

How many different sounds can you make with one **hand** on your desk?

Can you click your **fingers**?

Make up some short rhythms using any or all of these sounds.

4

Sound effects

Here are some things to do, using any of the sounds you think most suitable, with instruments, and with your body:—

Woodcutter chopping a tree

Oarsman rowing a boat

Railway engine starting off and vanishing into the distance

Birds fighting

The diesel roller at work

Children are walking in a wood. They see a fox; and run away

Rain falling in a pool

Journey to the moon

Midnight on the river

About rhythms

Have you ever *listened* to your feet on the pavement as you come to school?

Try a game with a friend. Shut your eyes, and tell your friend to do one of three things, walk, run, or skip along (not rope skipping!). You have to guess what he is doing.

Not very difficult, is it? Walking, running, skipping—each has a different sound.

Now take a percussion instrument and try to make it sound like walking, running, or skipping. Your friend has to guess which you are doing. If you get in a muddle you will have to go and listen to your feet on the ground once more.

6

About beats

The sound patterns we make when we walk, run, skip, or play a tambourine, are called *rhythms*.

When it is just a single pattern that goes on and on, like a clock ticking, or a runner running, or a bell chiming, we call it a *beat* or *pulse*. (Feel your own heart *beat*ing and feel the *pulse* in your own wrist.)

Try a game with beats. Count aloud, with your friend, up to twenty, then silently go on counting until you get to forty, or sixty, or even a hundred. The aim is to arrive on your final number exactly together. If you arrive at a hundred at the same moment you will do very well indeed.

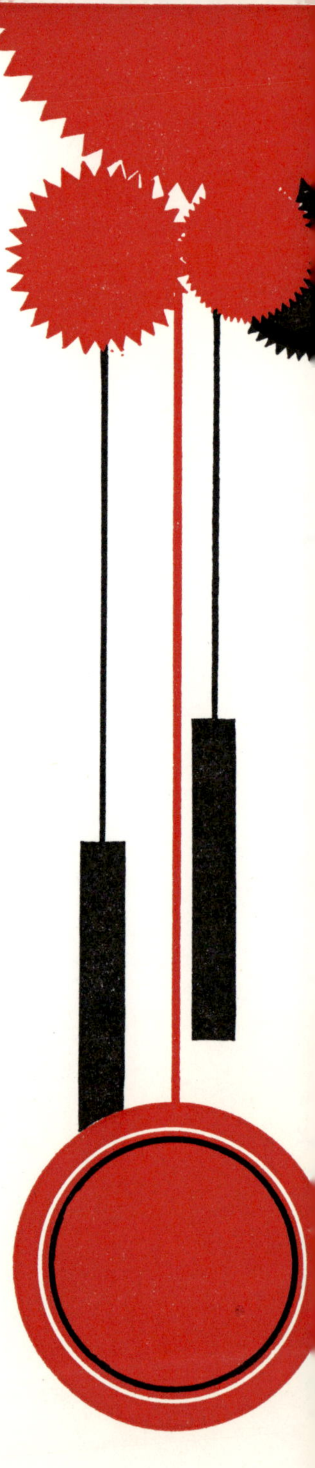

Beats and rhythms

When we walk we keep up a *beat* with our feet. But you do not like plain walking, do you? A skip and a jump and a run is much more fun.

In music it is the same. Music that walks all the time, runs all the time, or skips all the time is very likely to become dull to listen to. We need a mixture.

You will all know the song "Bobby Shaftoe". Most of the time it "runs", but not all the time. When does it "walk"?

Now take an instrument again, or clap. Make the sound of four walking steps, then four skipping steps, then four walking, four skipping, and so on.

Now do the same thing in threes, or fives, or twos.

Get your friend to sound the *skipping* steps at the time you are doing the *walking* ones, and then change over.

Do all these things with *walking* and *running* steps together.

Try this "Rhythm drama": A boy walks sadly along the road to school—his dog is ill. A girl skips up behind him and gives him a push. They have a race to school. They find that a pneumatic drill is digging a hole in the playground. The whistle goes. All the children run, walk or skip in to school. The drill stops. The man, in heavy boots, walks away to his hut for a cup of tea.

Make up your own "Rhythm Drama".

Rhythms with character

See if you can make up some rhythms which have character.

An angry rhythm and a gentle one.

A rhythm for an old man, and one for a child.

A jerky rhythm and a smooth one.

A rhythm for a bear and one for a monkey.

Play each rhythm by itself, and then try to fit each *pair* together.

Imagine these :—

An *angry* child with a *gentle* mother (or the other way round ?)

An old man walks with a child

A clown and a princess

A monkey teases a bear.

Rhythms of words

When we talk, the words we use make rhythm patterns. We do not think about this, of course, except when we say rhymes and jingles, and then we realise that they have a special kind of rhythm.

All words have their own rhythm. Try saying your own name—Christian name and Surname—four times running, and see if you can feel the rhythm of it.

Now play a guessing game with your friends: clap someone's name four times running, and see if the others can guess whose name it was.

Try the same game using the names of footballers, "Pop" singers, motor cars, aeroplanes, kings and queens of England, or anything else you can think of.

You will find that some rhythm patterns will fit more than one name. Which of these names have the same rhythm?

John Wood

Richard Jones

Bobby Johnson

David Wood

Gillian Richardson

Michael White

Rhythm quiz

See if you can tell which of these tunes have skipping rhythms in them, and which have running rhythms.

Sing a Song of Sixpence

Girls and Boys, come out to play

Baa-baa Black Sheep

Half a pound of twopenny rice

Humpty Dumpty

Here we go round the mulberry bush

Georgie Porgie

Hot Cross Buns.

A friend can help you in this way: he claps running rhythms, and you see which of the tunes will fit with his claps. Then do the same with skipping rhythms. All the tunes will fit one of the two rhythms. Write down your answers.

11

Making tunes

Why not try playing names and phrases on a xylophone (the one with wooden keys) or glockenspiel (with metal keys), or on a recorder, or even on a piano, if you have one?

Choose just one or two notes to start with—not necessarily "next-door" notes—and try playing your own name four times. Then try other notes. Find a tune for your own name that you can really remember. You can call this your "signature tune". If you use your surname as well, you will have a longer tune.

If some of your friends do this as well, you can have a "guess who" game.

Then play some proverbs (which are twice as long as most names) and have some more guessing games.

Here are some:—

Waste not, want not.

Too many cooks spoil the broth.

In for a penny, in for a pound.

Look before you leap.

Many hands make light work.

A bird in the hand is worth two in the bush.

Make hay while the sun shines.

12

More tune making

Take a proverb, say this one: Waste not, want not. Find two notes, G and E, and see how many *different* tunes you can make for this proverb, using only those two notes. Choose the one you like best, and try to remember it. Do the same with other proverbs.

Now play a game with your friend. First you choose three notes, say A, G, E, or G, E, D, or B, A, G; then you play a proverb on whichever three notes you choose, and he or she has to guess which it is, and play it back to you *exactly the same* as you played it. Take turns.

Now make a continuous tune. Take a proverb each, and play them backwards and forwards to each other without stopping. Do the same with a simple rhyme or jingle, taking one line each. Or make up your own short phrases about things that interest you.

Making a song

A song is a rhyme or poem which is sung instead of spoken.

If you sing a poem it becomes a song.

I saw a spider

Crawl–crawl–crawl.

I saw a spider

Crawling up the wall.

Say this, or any similar rhyme, to yourself lots of times, and see if you can persuade a tune to come and keep it company. (If you imagine the spider clearly it may help you to find a good tune.)

If you managed to find a tune for this rhyme, get a friend to accompany you, that is to say, play with you on an instrument. He or she could take a percussion instrument and play, whilst you sing the song.

Find other rhymes for yourself.

14

Making tunes on instruments

If you were not able to persuade a tune to come into your head for the "spider", try making up a tune for it on the glockenspiel or xylophone. At first do not allow yourself too many notes, or you may get muddled. Always try to sing as you play; after all, a song is for singing.

If you play the recorder, even if you have only just started, use that. Or if you have a piano try making up a tune on the black keys only, or some of them.

15

More tunes on instruments

Not all music has words, and you may want to make up tunes for instruments only—tunes to dance to, perhaps. But even if you are not going to sing the words, you will find them very useful for helping you to find tunes on your instruments. For instance this rhyme could help you to find a good tune for skipping or dancing:—

Turn the rope,
Turn the rope,
One, two, three;

Swing the rope,
Swing the rope,
Eight, nine, ten;

Skip the rope,
Skip the rope,
Turn the rope for me;

Twirl the rope,
Twirl the rope,
Over the rope again.

Find other rhymes with a good rhythm like this one.

When you have made a good tune, for this or any other rhyme, try playing it on other instruments. Perhaps you could teach it to some friends, and then play it three or four times, using different instruments each time, or two or three at once. Then add a little percussion.

16

Composing

Here are some useful things to remember when you are composing tunes:—

(a) Songs and instrumental pieces usually have sections, or phrases, that come more than once. For instance the tune we use for the phrase "Bobby Shaftoe's gone to sea" is exactly the same as the one we use for "He'll come back and marry me". So do not be afraid to repeat bits of your tunes—it usually makes them more "catchy" if you do.

(b) Do not think you have to have a different note for each syllable. "Twinkle, twinkle, little star" has two syllables for almost every note; the first three syllables of "Bobby Shaftoe" are all on one note; if you know the song "Dashing away with the smoothing iron" you will know that all the syllables of the refrain up to "Smooth-" are on one note—seven repeated notes.

(c) A "composed" tune is one that you remember.

If you have done some or all of the things suggested in this book you will have made up lots of tunes that you do not remember; but sometimes you will really want to compose tunes to remember. As you are doing it you will probably want to alter notes here and there until they sound just right, and make exactly the tune you want. Then the finished tune is your tune, and ready to be shared by the rest of your class. There is no reason why two people could not make up a tune together, so long as they agree on what sounds best.

17

Accompaniment

This long word means the same as "backing" on "pop" records. Most tunes sound better with some accompaniment. Before deciding on accompaniment to a song, you must read the words. Is there anything in the words that you could illustrate with an instrument? (Think of those sound effects.) Then you must decide what the character of the song is—lively, gentle, marching, funny—and think of a rhythm that suits it. Use this rhythm *all through the song*, repeating it again and again.

Take a song you know by heart. Some of you will sing it, whilst others make up and accompany the song on percussion instruments.

Take a great deal of trouble over accompaniments. They can make a great difference to a piece of music. Choose your instruments carefully. Make sure all of them can be heard. See that they all play important parts.

Words for songs

Words for songs are often much simpler than we imagine.
Here are some examples you may know. The repeated words
have been left out on purpose, so that you may see how very
simple the lines are:

1. Poor Jenny lies a-weeping

   On a fine summer's day.

2. Here we go round the mulberry bush

   On a cold and frosty morning.

3. Have you seen the muffin man

   Who lives in Drury Lane?

4. Lou, Lou, skip to my Lou

   Skip to my Lou, my darling.

5. John Brown had a little Indian

   One little Indian boy.

6. John Brown's body lies a-mouldering in the grave,

   But his soul goes marching on.

Do any of these pairs of lines rhyme?

When we make them into music we repeat words, or whole
lines, so that the music will seem to "rhyme". Thus, in numbers
4, 5 and 6, the first line is sung three times, and the last line
once. In each case lines one and three have exactly the same
tune.

See if you can describe the pattern in examples 1, 2 and 6.

Try making up some song words, and music, based on one
of these patterns.

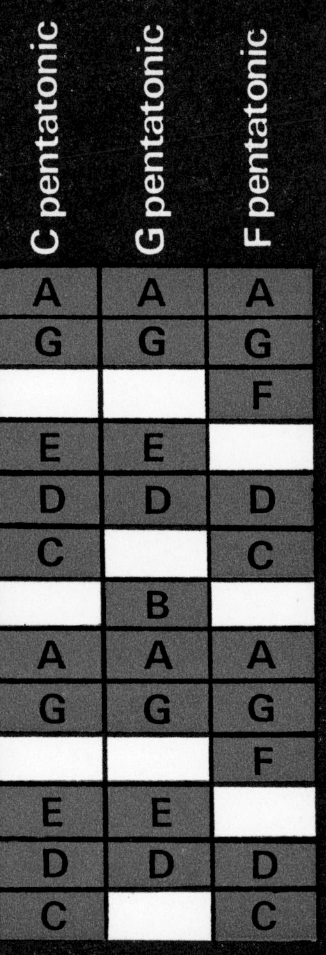

C pentatonic	G pentatonic	F pentatonic
A	A	A
G	G	G
		F
E	E	
D	D	D
C		C
	B	
A	A	A
G	G	G
		F
E	E	
D	D	D
C		C

19

Choosing notes

If you look at the letters on your xylophone you will find seven different ones before the first one returns. These are the seven notes of our scale.

Why is it that the eighth note has the same letter-name as the first?

It is because of the sound it makes. If you play two "C"s separately they sound different, but play them together and they sound almost like one note. (As a matter of fact the vibrations of the higher C are exactly twice as many as for the lower C, but men knew about the sounds long before they knew about the vibrations.)

Now play the scale from C to C, upwards (that is, starting at the wider end of the instrument), singing the notes to "Doh ray me fah soh lah te doh"—the singing names we give to the notes of our scale.

Next, take off notes F and B (fah and te) and play the notes that are left. You will find that having gaps in your scale will help you to find your way about the xylophone. It also gives us a scale that many (unknown) composers of folk tunes have found quite satisfactory.

You now have five different notes in your scale—Doh ray me— soh lah—doh ray me—and so on.

That time we called C doh. But any note can be doh.

This time we will call F doh.

Put back all the notes, and then take away fah and te (in this case B and E) and try again. Take away also the te (E) below doh (F).

Now put back all the notes and do the same again, using G as doh.

These 5-note scales we call by a long name—Pentatonic. Quite a lot of folk songs use only the notes of the pentatonic scale.

Try playing "L'il Liza Jane" (if you know it) using the C pentatonic scale—the tune begins on E (me).

Try playing "Auld Lang Syne" using the F pentatonic scale—this tune begins on bottom soh (C).

Experiments with scales

You have tried three pentatonic scales, beginning on C, F, and G. Now get a friend to play one of them to you, and see if you can tell which of the three it is, without looking.

Do not worry if you cannot tell the difference, for in fact all three do sound the same, except that each is at a different level of pitch. The reason for this is that the distance, or *interval*, between each note of this pentatonic and its neighbour is the same in each of the three scales. For this reason also we give the notes the same "singing names"—Doh ray me—soh lah—doh—in each scale.

But if you think that *every* note on your xylophone is the same distance in sound from its neighbour, you are mistaken.

To prove it try playing the 5-note scale beginning on D;— D E F—A B—D. Play it up and down several times, and compare it with the C pentatonic. One of the five notes sounds different. Which? If you do not agree as to the answer, discuss it with your teacher.

There is no reason whatever why we should not use the D 5-note scale, or any other, if we happen to like the sound of it, or if it suits the *mood* of the music we are composing.

Play both the C and the D 5-note scales once more, and then consider which of the two would be more suitable for (a) A gay dance (b) A Soldiers' March (c) A funeral march (d) A witch's Sabbath.

There are no "right" answers to these questions—your opinion is as good as anybody else's. Composers of different periods have felt differently about them.

Use any of these scales in your tune-making games, or in your composing. Take away the notes you do not need.

If your xylophone is big enough, try the 5-note scale beginning on A. Use that also.

21

More about rhythm and words

We have already seen that proverbs can be said, or sung, in both "skipping" and "running" rhythms.

So every time we find a rhyme we wish to use for making a song, the first thing we have to decide is what kind of rhythm we shall use.

Sometimes the choice is very easy:—

Marching in our wellingtons,
Tramp, tramp, tramp,
Marching in our wellingtons
We won't get damp.

Splashing through the puddles
In the rain, rain, rain,
Splashing through the puddles,
And splashing home again.

Swing me over the water
Swing me over the sea
Swing me over the garden wall
And swing me home to tea.

Each of these has such a natural rhythm of its own that we need not spend long wondering which kind of rhythm to use.

But sometimes it could well be either, as in this one:—

London bridge is broken down,
Broken down, broken down,
London bridge is broken down,
My fair lady.

Try to *say* this rhyme using "running" rhythms first, then using "skipping" rhythms. You have to decide which you prefer.

Pieces for instruments

Here are a few ideas for you to make up some pieces for instruments only.

Dance of the Skeletons

Cowboys' Gallop

Evening on the River

Guy Fawkes

Hallowe'en

Christmas Dance of the Shepherds

Ghosts

Musical descriptions of people you know.

Try making up a story, with music to describe people, animals, or incidents in it.

23

Speed

Perhaps you have not yet tried any games with speed, so here are a few suggestions.

Make up a little tune. Now play it *very slowly* and repeat it again and again, getting faster and faster all the time.

Do the same, starting very fast, and slowing down.

Make some music:

(a)   For machinery starting and stopping.

(b)   People are walking along a street when it begins to rain. As it rains harder the people walk faster, and then run for shelter, till no one is left on the street.

Now take a tune that everybody knows, and see if you can play it, or sing it, so slowly that nobody recognises it.

What instruments in your classroom would be most suitable for a slow melody?

Using two melody instruments make up two tunes which sound together. Call it "A jester tries to make the sad king happy".

Make up some music for a mouse and a lion. Use the same five notes for each, but make their tunes as different as can be. If you know the fable by Aesop about the mouse who freed the lion, you could use your music to illustrate the story.

Finally make up a little signature tune for yourself. Play it in three different ways:—(1) when you are happy (2) when you are sad (3) when you are angry.

Twos and threes

So far we have tried only "running" and "skipping" rhythms.

Let us take a phrase, "Skipping is *fun*".

Start clapping its rhythm fast, and gradually slow it down until it is quite slow. Now can you count

"one–two–three–one–two–three"

quite evenly whilst you are doing it?

You have probably sung a few songs that can be counted in threes. See if you can say which of these songs are in twos, and which in threes. One person counts while the other sings :–

God save the Queen

The Drunken Sailor

Charlie is me darling

Poor Jenny lies a-weeping

Skip to my Lou

25

More about "three time"

Sometimes a rhyme is not set to music in the most natural way it could be. Instead syllables are "stretched" to fit a beat that goes in threes—one-two-three-one-two-three—instead of the more common "two" grouping.

In the song "Poor Jenny lies a-weeping" the syllable "Jen-" is stretched far longer than it would be in speech.

In the carol "The Holly and the Ivy" the two words "and the" are stretched, or slowed down—if you said them you would say those two little words very quickly.

Which words are lengthened in "God save the Queen"?

Any rhyme, whether in "skipping" or "running" rhythm, can be stretched into a three-beat grouping. In this rhyme: "Jeremiah blow the fire, Puff puff puff" if you stretch the "Jer-", the "blow", the first "puff", the third "puff", you will fit it into a three-beat count easily. First establish your beat by giving one slap on the desk, and two with hands together— all even beats—then say the poem whilst you are doing it.

More experiments with scales

You may be wanting those notes, fah and te, which we have not used in our pentatonic tunes, so let us put them all on.

Start on C and play up all the notes to the top of the xylophone, singing their names, doh ray etc. Then come down again.

Now call F doh, and start your scale again, this time on F. Climb up and down. Does any note sound "odd"?

If it does, change it with one of the spare notes you should have with your instrument. (In the case of the recorder you will have to find out the fingering of the new note.) Find the note that sounds right for the scale of F.

If you compose a piece using the notes in the scale of C, we say the piece is in the *key* of C. If you change the spare note to suit the scale of F, then your key is now F.

You can now try for yourself the scale of G.

All these three keys can be used on your xylophone, and if there were enough "spare" notes you could use 12 different keys altogether.

Other scales

Do you remember the pentatonic scale you tried beginning on D? And also the one beginning on A?

Now try the complete scales beginning on D—Ray me fah soh lah te doh ray etc. and down again,

and the complete scale beginning on A—lah te doh ray me fah soh lah.

These two scales sound rather different from the C, G and F ones, and also from each other. We give them different names:—the ray *mode* and the lah *mode*. A tune using the ray mode must end on ray, and a lah mode piece must end on lah.

"The Drunken Sailor" is a ray mode tune—it begins on lah (A) and of course ends on ray. Try to play it.

"The Raggle taggle gypsies" is a lah mode tune—it begins on me (E) and of course ends on lah.

If you like these two modes, use them for your own compositions.

Two or more notes at once

Take two sticks and try the effect of two notes together.
First on a xylophone, then on a glockenspiel.

Try all sort of pairs of notes, and decide which pairs you like
the sound of, and which you don't.

Do the two sounds of the different instruments make any
difference to your choice?

Next, you will need someone to help you, for you are going
to try the effect of three notes sounding together. Try all
sorts of combinations, and see if you can find those that please
you and those that don't.

Notes that sound together like this we call chords.

Using chords try to make up some music for a stately
procession.

Chords are often used as accompaniment to a melody.

Make some music for a young man cheerfully whistling as he
walks to work. His "walking" will be made with a chord (or
two, in turns) on one instrument, while his "whistling" could
be made on a recorder, or just whistling.

A "broken" chord is one in which the notes are not sounded
all together. It gives a smoother effect.

Make some music for a boat on a river. Use a *broken chord*
for the water (on a suitable instrument), and let your *tune*
tell the listener what kind of a boat it is.

Harmonizing

Think of a simple song, say "Frère Jacques". Prepare your glockenspiel for the key of G, and sound Doh. Then, while your friend is singing the tune, you have to try and find a pair of notes which fit if you play them on the beat—that is, on the underlined syllables:—

Frère Jacques, Frère Jacques,

Dormez-vous, dormez-vous?

and so on.

When you have found two notes that will fit well with the tune, try and add a third note.

Do the same thing for:

The Holly and the Ivy (Key G)

Row, row, row the boat (Key C)

Li'l Liza Jane (Key C)

Little David, play on your harp (Key G)

30

Changing chord

If you have discovered the trick you are ready for the next stage.

Take one of these songs:

Cockles and Mussels

Clementine

Polly-wolly-doodle

Ten Green Bottles

Prepare the key of G, and your first *chord*—the name we give to a group of notes played together—and then ask your friend to sing whilst you play on the strong beats only (every other beat). When you feel that your two notes no longer fit with the tune, stop playing, and find two notes that *will* fit with that part of the tune. Carry on until the end, stopping if you need to change.

You may find this hard at first, but you will soon get practised at it.

We call this "harmonizing" a tune, and it makes a nice addition to your "backing."

It is a comparatively new idea—only a few hundred years old (which is little when you think of how long people have been making music)—and musicians in some Eastern countries still prefer to use melody only.

There are innumerable ways of harmonizing a tune, but if you can "feel" when you need to change chord, and change in whatever simple way you have discovered, you will have made a very good start.

31

Making a round

Two of you play a three-note chord on a glockenspiel, and keep playing it in regular beats—the notes could be F A C.

A third person, or two others taking it in turns, make up a tune by *singing* this verse (or any other like it), trying again and again until they are sure that their melody fits with the chord.

Jeremiah, blow the fire,

Puff, puff, puff!

First you blow it gently,

Then you blow it rough.

Try *not* to let the melody repeat itself. If you do, the different groups, when they sing it as a round, will find themselves singing the same tune as each other.

Instrumentation

Let us suppose that you have in your classroom a variety of melody instruments, say recorders, xylophone and glockenspiel at least.

Any tune will sound different when played on another instrument.

Take any tune—your own or someone else's—and play it three times, using a different instrument each time. Then, with the help of a friend or two, try combinations of instruments together. How many different combinations are possible with three instruments?

Perhaps you could play part of the tune on one instrument, and the rest on another. In this way you could have as much variety as you like.

If you can harmonize a little as well, you have even more possibilities for different combinations. For instance;

1st time	Melody—glockenspiel
	Harmony—recorders
2nd time	Melody—recorders
	Harmony—xylophone
3rd time	Melody—glockenspiel
	Harmony—xylophone

How many more combinations can you think of?

You could also have many percussion instruments, which could be varied as much as you like. There is no end to what you can do.

We call this choosing of different instruments "Instrumentation". It is an excellent way of making a short piece longer, for, by changing instruments, we can repeat tunes without their becoming monotonous.

33

Some more ideas

Descants. When you have composed a tune, try playing exactly the same tune "in parallel" with it or, if you like, "holding hands" with it; it could be any number of notes away from the original tune. See which you like best when you play the "original" and the parallel" together.

It will not *always* sound good, but it may sometimes.

Sequences. Compose a little phrase, about as long as a name rhythm. Make it start on C. Repeat it one note higher, beginning on D, then again, beginning on E, and so on until you get tired of it.

A sequence of about three steps—sometimes less, sometimes more—often occurs in tunes. It can go up or down by steps. Keep a look out for an example.

Steps and leaps. If you are composing at a xylophone, get into the habit of using two sticks. You will usually get better tunes if you make the notes go by big interval jumps (e.g.

from C to F or A) sometimes and by scale (i.e. next door notes) sometimes—a mixture of jumps and steps in other words. Much will depend on the mood.

Longer tunes. A great many tunes last quite a long time, but when you really listen to them you find that much of it is repetition. A "Pop" tune lasting three minutes would probably last about half a minute if you cut out all the repetition.

A simple way of making your tunes last longer is to repeat them. But it may become monotonous if you do not make some slight change with every repetition—add an instrument, change instruments, play it an octave higher, make it louder, or softer.

Another way to make a longer tune is to have at least *two* musical ideas; then you can extend them by repeating them in any order you choose, and making alterations.

This is the kind of thing to do in groups. One group makes up a tune for, say, a march—a tune of 16 beats.

When this is done everyone listens to it carefully a few times, and then another group makes up a second tune, not the same, but not too different in mood. When completed you can play the tunes through something like this:—tune "A" played twice, tune "B" played twice, tune "A" played twice. Or you could make up your own repetition scheme. Tune "B" could be in a different key if you liked.

If you had three tunes you would have even more scope for varying your repetitions.

34

Using your instruments

Try to make each instrument have music that really suits it, and suits the player.

See how many sounds you can get from a xylophone that you could not possibly get from a recorder or a singer.

Which instruments can play big jumps easily, and which cannot?

Sometimes you could compose a tune on the xylophone, and then make a different version of the same tune to suit the glockenspiel or recorder.

How many things can you do with your voice that you cannot do on instruments?

Conclusion

In the world of music you can find songs and instrumental pieces about almost anything you can think of.

And music also expresses what you think and feel about things, people, or events.

So make up music about anything that is going on, at home or in school, that really interests you, for that is what other people will like to hear.